Do Not Spill!

By Megan Albrecht   Illustrated by Pamela Leavens

Target Skill Review

PEARSON

Scott
Foresman

Dan and Tim will set up a stand.
Mom and Dad will help.

Dan and Tim get the cups.

Mom and Dad set up the stand.

Tim will fill it up.

Do not spill, Tim.

Dan will mix it.

Do not spill, Dan.

Lin said, "Will you fill up my cup?"
Do not spill, Tim.

Meg said, "Will you fill up my cup?"
Do not spill, Dan.

Dan and Tim have fun at the stand.
They did not spill.